Essential Christmas Prayers

PARACLETE PRESS

PARACLETE PRESS
BREWSTER, MASSACHUSETTS

2017 First Printing
Essential Christmas Prayers
Copyright © 2017 by Paraclete Press, Inc.
ISBN 978-1-61261-969-9

Library of Congress Cataloging-in-Publication Data

Names: Paraclete Press.
Title: Essential Christmas prayers.
Description: Brewster, Massachusetts : Paraclete Press Inc., 2017.
Identifiers: LCCN 2017028329 | ISBN 9781612619699 (trade paper)
Subjects: LCSH: Christmas—Prayers and devotions. | Carols, English.
Classification: LCC BV45 .E87 2017 | DDC 242/.335—dc23
LC record available at https://lccn.loc.gov/2017028329

10 9 8 7 6 5 4 3 2 1

Published by Paraclete Press
Brewster, Massachusetts
www.paracletepress.com

Printed in the United States of America

Contents

Essential Christmas Prayers

$\mathcal{I}$ntroduction

The Christmas season speaks not only of God coming to earth, becoming human, and living among us, but of the dream of peace on earth and good will toward all people. We feel the call to be kinder to each other—to be a little friendlier, a little more generous.

Some prayers we say at church; some prayers we say at home. Some we say at a particular time of day, some on a particular day of the year, and some prayers we say whenever we are moved to reach out to God. What follows is a collection of beloved and beautiful prayers for the Christmas season and Advent. Some were written by saints, some by hymn and liturgy writers . . . and one was written by an astronaut.

Christmas Prayer from Space

Apollo 8 astronaut Frank Borman was scheduled as a reader for the Christmas Day service at his church, St. Christopher's Episcopal Church in League City, Texas, when the launch time was changed and he found he'd be in space on that day. He worked with fellow congregant Rod Rose on a new prayer he could read to the world. Borman read the following prayer from space while circling the moon on Christmas Day, 1968.

Give us, O God, the vision which can see your love
in the world in spite of human failure.

Give us the faith to trust your goodness in spite of
our ignorance and weakness.

Give us the knowledge that we may continue to
pray with understanding hearts.

And show us what each one of us can do to set
forward the coming of the day of universal peace.

Bidding Prayer for Christmastide

The Festival of Nine Lessons and Carols at the Chapel of King's College, Cambridge, has changed very little since 1918. Its dean at that time, Eric Milner-White, wrote parts of the service, including this beloved bidding prayer, which is used widely today.

Beloved in Christ,
this Christmastide, it is our duty and delight
to prepare ourselves to hear again the message of the angels,
and to go in heart and mind to Bethlehem,
and see this thing which is come to pass,
and the Babe lying in a manger.

Therefore let us hear again from Holy Scripture
the tale of the loving purposes of God from the first days of
     our sin
until the glorious redemption brought us by this holy Child;
and let us make this house of prayer glad with our carols of
     praise.

But first, because this of all things would rejoice Jesus' heart,
let us pray to him for the needs of the whole world, and all
     his people;
for peace upon the earth he came to save;
for love and unity within the one Church he did build;
for goodwill among all peoples.

And particularly at this time let us remember
the poor, the cold, the hungry, the oppressed;
the sick and them that mourn; the lonely and the unloved;
the aged and the little children;
and all who know not the Lord Jesus, or who love him not,
or who by sin have grieved his heart of love.

Lastly, let us remember all those who rejoice with us,
but upon another shore and in a greater light,
that multitude which no one can number,
whose hope was in the Word made flesh,
and with whom, in this Lord Jesus, we for evermore are one.

Moonless Darkness
BY GERARD MANLEY HOPKINS

Moonless darkness stands between.
Past, the Past, no more be seen!
But the Bethlehem star may lead me
To the sight of Him Who freed me
From the self that I have been.
Make me pure, Lord: Thou art Holy;
Make me meek, Lord: Thou wert lowly;
Now beginning, and always,
Now begin, on Christmas day.
(1865)

Love Came Down at Christmas
BY CHRISTINA ROSSETTI

This nineteenth-century poem by Christina Rossetti[1] has been used as a prayer and set to music many times, including by the Anglican composer John Rutter and the band Jars of Clay.

Love came down at Christmas,
Love all lovely, Love Divine,
Love was born at Christmas,
Star and Angels gave the sign.

Worship we the Godhead,
Love Incarnate, Love Divine,
Worship we our Jesus,
But wherewith for sacred sign?

Love shall be our token,
Love be yours and love be mine,
Love to God and all men,
Love for plea and gift and sign.

Excerpt from a Children's Carol
BY MARTIN LUTHER

Martin Luther wrote "Vom Himmel hoch da komm ich her" for his infant son Hans as a carol for Christmas Eve, 1540. The first half of the song is from the perspective of the angel in Luke 2:10 delivering the news of Jesus's birth. The second half is our response to the news, and it has become a beloved Christmas prayer. This translation of the second half, one of many, is by Catherine Winkworth.[2]

> Ah, Lord, who hast created all,
> How hast Thou made Thee weak and small,
> That Thou must choose Thy infant bed
> Where ass and ox but lately fed!
>
> Were earth a thousand times as fair,
> Beset with gold and jewels rare,
> She yet were far too poor to be
> A narrow cradle, Lord, for Thee.
>
> For velvets soft and silken stuff
> Thou hast but hay and straw so rough,
> Whereon Thou King, so rich and great,
> As 'twere Thy heaven, art throned in state.

Thus hath it pleased Thee to make plain
The truth to us poor fools and vain,
That this world's honor, wealth, and might
Are naught and worthless in Thy sight.

Ah! dearest Jesus, Holy Child,
Make Thee a bed, soft, undefiled,
Within my heart, that it may be
A quiet chamber kept for Thee.

My heart for very joy doth leap,
My lips no more can silence keep;
I too must sing with joyful tongue
That sweetest ancient cradle-song—

Glory to God in highest Heaven,
Who unto man His Son hath given!
While angels sing with pious mirth
A glad New Year to all the earth.

A Christmas Prayer for the Home
BY HENRY VAN DYKE

The following prayer was penned by Henry van Dyke and included in the book *The Spirit of Christmas* in 1905.[3] This version uses slightly modernized wording.

Father of all humankind, look upon our family,
Kneeling together before you,
And grant us a true Christmas.

With loving heart, we bless you:
For the gift of your dear Son, Jesus Christ,
For the peace he brings to our homes,
For the goodwill he teaches to sinful humankind,
For the glory of your goodness shining in his face.

With joyful voice, we praise you:
For his lowly birth and his resting in the manger,
For the pure tenderness of his mother, Mary,
For the fatherly care that protected him,
For the Providence that saved the holy Child
To be the Savior of the world.

With deep desire, we beseech you:
Help us to keep his birthday truly,
Help us to offer, in his name, our Christmas prayer.

Essential Christmas Prayers

From the sickness of sin and the darkness of doubt,
From selfish pleasures and sullen pains,
From the frost of pride and the fever of envy,
God save us every one, through the blessing of Jesus.

In the health of purity and the calm of mutual trust,
In the sharing of joy and the bearing of trouble,
In the steady glow of love and the clear light of hope,
God keep us every one, by the blessing of Jesus.

In praying and praising, in giving and receiving,
In eating and drinking, in singing and making merry,
In parents' gladness and in children's mirth,
In dear memories of those who have departed,
In good comradeship with those who are here,
In kind wishes for those who are far away,
In patient waiting, sweet contentment, generous cheer,
God bless us every one, with the blessing of Jesus.

By remembering our kinship with all people,
By well-wishing, friendly speaking, and kindly doing,
By cheering the downcast and adding sunshine to daylight,
By welcoming strangers (poor shepherds or wise men),
By keeping the music of the angels' song in this home,
God help us every one to share the blessing of Jesus,

In whose name we keep Christmas,
And in whose words we pray together:

Our Father who art in heaven, hallowed be thy name.
Thy kingdom come. Thy will be done in earth,
as it is in heaven.
Give us this day our daily bread. And forgive us our debts,
as we forgive our debtors.
And lead us not into temptation, but deliver us from evil:
For thine is the kingdom, and the power, and the glory,
forever and ever.
Amen.

A Christmas Prayer for the Lonely Folks
BY HENRY VAN DYKE

Here is another Christmas prayer from Henry van Dyke's book *The Spirit of Christmas*.[4]

Lord God of the solitary,
Look upon me in my loneliness.
Since I may not keep this Christmas in the home,
Send it into my heart.

Do not let my sins cloud me in,
But shine through them with forgiveness in the face of the
    child Jesus.
Put me in loving remembrance of the lowly lodging in the
    stable of Bethlehem,
The sorrows of the blessed Mary, the poverty and exile of the
    Prince of Peace.
For his sake, give me cheerful courage to endure my lot,
And inward comfort to sweeten it.

Purge my heart from hard and bitter thoughts.
Let no shadow of forgetting come between me and friends
    far away;
Bless them in their Christmas mirth.
Hedge me in with faithfulness,
That I may not grow unworthy to meet them again.

Give me good work to do,
So that I may forget myself and find peace in doing it for you.
Though I am poor, send me to carry some gift to those who
are poorer,
Some cheer to those who are lonelier.
Grant me the joy to do a kindness to one of your little ones:
Light my Christmas candle at the gladness of an innocent
and grateful heart.

Strange is the path where you lead me:
Let me not doubt your wisdom, nor lose your hand.
Make me sure that Eternal Love is revealed in Jesus, your
dear Son,
To save us from sin and solitude and death.
Teach me that I am not alone,
But that many hearts all around the world
Join with me through the silence while I pray in his name:

Our Father who art in heaven, hallowed be thy name.
Thy kingdom come. Thy will be done in earth,
as it is in heaven.
Give us this day our daily bread. And forgive us our debts,
as we forgive our debtors.
And lead us not into temptation, but deliver us from evil:
For thine is the kingdom, and the power, and the glory,
forever and ever.
Amen.

Essential Christmas Prayers

Loving Mother of the Redeemer

Known in Latin as "Alma Redemptoris Mater," this prayer is attributed to Hermannus Contractus (1013–1054) and traditionally recited before bed (at Compline) during Advent and Christmas.

Loving Mother of the Redeemer,
gate of heaven, star of the sea,
assist your people who have fallen
yet strive to rise again.
To the wonderment of nature you bore your Creator,
yet remained a virgin after as before.
You who received Gabriel's joyful greeting,
have pity on us poor sinners.

A Little Child of Love
BY EDWARD BOUVERIE PUSEY

Edward Bouverie Pusey (1800–1882) was an Anglican priest and became the leader of the Oxford movement, which eventually evolved into Anglo-Catholicism.

Good Jesus,
born at this time,
a little child of love for us;
be born in me
so that I may be
a little child in love with you.

Prayers for
Lighting of the Weekly
Candles in
Advent

First Sunday of Advent

Stir up thy power, O Lord, and come,
that by thy protection we may be rescued
from the dangers that beset us through our sins;
and be a Redeemer to deliver us;
Who lives and reigns with God the Father
in the unity of the Holy Spirit, one God forever and ever.
Amen.

Second Sunday of Advent

Stir up our hearts, O Lord,
to prepare the paths of thine Only-begotten Son:
that we may worthily serve thee
with hearts purified by His coming:
Who lives and reigns with God the Father
in the unity of the Holy Spirit, one God forever and ever.
Amen

Third Sunday of Advent

We beseech thee to listen to our prayers, O Lord,
and by the grace of thy coming enlighten our darkened minds:
Thou who lives and reigns with God the Father
in the unity of the Holy Spirit, one God forever and ever.
Amen.

Fourth Sunday of Advent

Pour forth thy power, O Lord, and come:
Assist us by that mighty power,
so that by thy grace and merciful kindness
we may swiftly receive the salvation that our sins impede:
Who lives and reigns with God the Father
in the unity of the Holy Spirit, one God forever and ever.
Amen.

Other Prayers for Advent

Dear Infant Jesus,
In a short time
You will come
To visit us,
And your holy, divine coming
Is full of peace, joy, and love.
Our hearts are full of your love
In our daily life.
Dear Jesus, please help
All your devotees
Around the world.
Thanks, my dear Lord.

Lord, raise up, we pray thee, thy power, and come among us, and with great might succor us; that whereas, through our sins and wickedness, we are sore let and hindered in running the race that is set before us, thy bountiful grace and mercy may speedily help and deliver us; through Jesus Christ our Lord, to whom, with thee and the Holy Ghost, be honor and glory, world without end. Amen.[5]

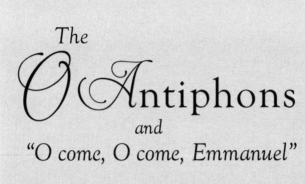

The
O Antiphons
and
"O come, O come, Emmanuel"

We're not certain when the O Antiphons were written—possibly as early as the fifth century—but we do know that by the eighth or ninth century, Christians across Western Europe were turning to them every Advent. Traditionally, the seven short prayers are chanted one a day from December 17 through December 23, each addressing Christ by one of his names, or attributes. They are called the "O Antiphons" of course, because they are antiphons—short songs that precede longer pieces such as psalms—and they all begin with the word "O," the archaic form of "Oh."

O Sapientia

O Sapientia, quae ex ore Altissimi prodiisti,
attingens a fine usque ad finem,
fortiter suaviterque disponens omnia:
veni ad docendum nos viam prudentiae.

O Wisdom,

O Holy Word of God,

You govern all creation with your strong, yet tender care:

Come, and show your people the way to salvation.

O Adonai

O Adonai, et Dux domus Israel,
qui Moysi in igne flammae rubi apparuisti,
et ei in Sina legem dedisti:
veni ad redimendum nos in brachio extento.

O Sacred Lord of ancient Israel,

Who showed yourself to Moses in the burning bush,

Who gave him the holy law on Sinai mountain:

Come, stretch out your mighty hand to set us free.

O Radix Jesse

O Radix Jesse, qui stas in signum populorum,
super quem continebunt reges os suum,
quem Gentes deprecabuntur:
veni ad liberandum nos, jam noli tardare.

O Flower of Jesse's stem,
You have been raised up as a sign for all peoples;
Kings stand silent in your presence;
The nations bow down in worship before you:
Come, let nothing keep you from coming to our aid.

O Clavis David

O Clavis David, et sceptrum domus Israel;
qui aperis, et nemo claudit;
claudis, et nemo aperit:
veni, et educ vinctum de domo carceris,
sedentem in tenebris, et umbra mortis.

O Key of David,
O Royal Power of Israel,
Controlling at your will the gate of heaven:
Come, break down the prison walls of death
For those who dwell in darkness and the shadow of death;
And lead your captive people into freedom.

O Oriens

O Oriens,
splendor lucis aeternae, et sol justitiae:
veni, et illumina sedentes in tenebris, et umbra mortis.

O Radiant Dawn,
Splendor of eternal light,
Sun of justice:
Come, shine on those who dwell in darkness
And the shadow of death.

O Rex Gentium

O Rex Gentium, et desideratus earum,
lapisque angularis, qui facis utraque unum:
veni, et salva hominem,
quem de limo formasti.

O King of all the nations,
The only joy of every human heart:
O Keystone of the mighty arch of man:
Come and save the creature you fashioned from the dust.

Essential Christmas Prayers

O Emmanuel

O Emmanuel, Rex et legifer noster,
exspectatio Gentium, et Salvator earum:
veni ad salvandum nos, Domine, Deus noster.

O Emmanuel,
King and Lawgiver,
Desire of the nations,
Savior of all people:
Come and set us free, Lord, our God!

O come, O come, Emmanuel

This anonymous prayer song from the twelfth century is the definitive Advent hymn. The familiar English translation from the Latin is by John Mason Neale in 1851.

> O come, O come, Emmanuel,
> And ransom captive Israel,
> That mourns in lonely exile here
> Until the Son of God appear.
> *Rejoice! Rejoice!*
> *Emmanuel shall come to thee, O Israel.*
>
> O come, thou Wisdom from on high,
> Who order all things far and nigh;
> To us the path of knowledge show,
> And teach us in her ways to go.
> *Rejoice! Rejoice!*
> *Emmanuel shall come to thee, O Israel.*
>
> O come, thou Day-spring, come and cheer
> Our spirits by thine advent here;
> Disperse the gloomy clouds of night,
> And death's dark shadows put to right.
> *Rejoice! Rejoice!*
> *Emmanuel shall come to thee, O Israel.*

O come, O come, great Lord of might,
Who to thy tribes on Sinai's height
In ancient times once gave the law
In cloud and majesty and awe.
Rejoice! Rejoice!
Emmanuel shall come to thee, O Israel.

O come, Desire of nations, bind
In one the hearts of all mankind;
Bid thou our sad divisions cease,
And be thyself our King of Peace.
Rejoice! Rejoice!
Emmanuel shall come to thee, O Israel.

O come, O come, Emmanuel
—ANOTHER VERSION

While the version above is the one most people know, this translation by T. A. Lacey (1853–1931)[6] more clearly shows the link between "O Come, O Come, Emmanuel" and the O Antiphons.

O come, O come, Emmanuel!
Redeem thy captive Israel,
That into exile drear is gone
Far from the face of God's dear Son.
Rejoice! Rejoice! Emmanuel
Shall come to thee, O Israel.

O come, thou Wisdom from on high!
Who madest all in earth and sky,
Creating man from dust and clay:
To us reveal salvation's way.
Rejoice! Rejoice! Emmanuel
Shall come to thee, O Israel.

O come, O come, Adonai,
Who in thy glorious majesty
From Sinai's mountain, clothed with awe,
Gavest thy folk the ancient law.
Rejoice! Rejoice! Emmanuel
Shall come to thee, O Israel.

Essential Christmas Prayers

O come, thou Root of Jesse! draw
The quarry from the lion's claw;
From those dread caverns of the grave,
From nether hell, thy people save.
Rejoice! Rejoice! Emmanuel
Shall come to thee, O Israel.

O come, thou Lord of David's Key!
The royal door fling wide and free;
Safeguard for us the heavenward road,
And bar the way to death's abode.
Rejoice! Rejoice! Emmanuel
Shall come to thee, O Israel.

O come, O come, thou Dayspring bright!
Pour on our souls thy healing light;
Dispel the long night's lingering gloom,
And pierce the shadows of the tomb.
Rejoice! Rejoice! Emmanuel
Shall come to thee, O Israel.

O come, Desire of nations! show
Thy kingly reign on earth below;
Thou Cornerstone, uniting all,
Restore the ruin of our fall.
Rejoice! Rejoice! Emmanuel
Shall come to thee, O Israel.

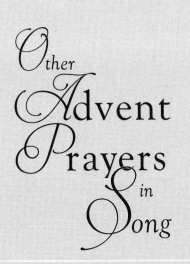

Other
Advent
Prayers
in
Song

Sometimes prayers are put to music and become songs, or in the case of Advent prayers, hymns. Here are a few other beloved Advent prayer songs.

Come, Thou Long-Expected Jesus

This Advent hymn was written by Charles Wesley in 1745.

Come, thou long-expected Jesus,
Born to set thy people free;
From our fears and sins release us;
Let us find our rest in thee.

Israel's Strength and Consolation,
Hope of all the earth thou art;
Dear Desire of every nation,
Joy of every longing heart.

Born thy people to deliver,
Born a child and yet a King,
Born to reign in us forever,
Now thy gracious kingdom bring.

By thine own eternal Spirit
Rule in all our hearts alone;
By thine all-sufficient merit
Raise us to thy glorious throne.

Come, Thou Redeemer of the Earth

St. Ambrose of Milan (340–397) penned this Advent hymn.
The English translation is by John Mason Neale (1818-1866).

Come, Thou Redeemer of the earth,
And manifest Thy virgin birth:
Let every age adoring fall;
Such birth befits the God of all.
Begotten of no human will,
But of the Spirit, Thou art still
The Word of God in flesh arrayed,
The promised Fruit to man displayed.

The virgin womb that burden gained
With virgin honor all unstained;
The banners there of virtue glow;
God in His temple dwells below.
Forth from His chamber goeth He,
That royal home of purity,
A giant in twofold substance one,
Rejoicing now His course to run.

From God the Father He proceeds,
To God the Father back He speeds;
His course He runs to death and hell,
Returning on God's throne to dwell.
O equal to the Father, Thou!
Gird on Thy fleshly mantle now;
The weakness of our mortal state
With deathless might invigorate.

Thy cradle here shall glitter bright,
And darkness breathe a newer light,
Where endless faith shall shine serene,
And twilight never intervene.
All laud to God the Father be;
All praise, eternal Son, to Thee;
All glory, as is ever meet,
To God the Holy Paraclete.

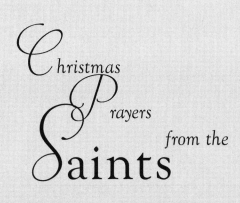

Christmas Prayers from the Saints

St. Andrew the Apostle

(B. EARLY 1ST CENTURY AD)

Some pray the St. Andrew Christmas Novena, also called simply the Christmas Novena, fifteen times a day from the Feast of St. Andrew the Apostle on November 30 until Christmas.

> Hail and blessed be the hour and moment
> in which the Son of God was born
> of the most pure virgin Mary,
> at midnight,
> in Bethlehem,
> in the piercing cold.
> In that hour vouchsafe, I beseech thee, O my God,
> to hear my prayer and grant my desires,
> through the merits of Our Savior, Jesus Christ,
> and of His Blessed Mother.
> Amen.

St. Ephraim the Syrian
(AD 306–373)

The feast day of your birth resembles You, Lord,
Because it brings joy to all humanity.
Old people and infants alike enjoy your day.
Your day is celebrated
From generation to generation.
Kings and emperors may pass away,
And the festivals to commemorate them soon lapse.
But your festival
Will be remembered until the end of time.
Your day is a means and a pledge of peace.
At your birth heaven and earth were reconciled,
Since you came from heaven to earth on that day.
You forgave our sins and wiped away our guilt.
You gave us so many gifts on the day of your birth:
A treasure chest of spiritual medicines for the sick;
Spiritual light for the blind;
The cup of salvation for the thirsty;
The bread of life for the hungry.
In the winter when trees are bare,
You give us the most succulent spiritual fruit.
In the frost when the earth is barren,
You bring new hope to our souls.
In December when seeds are hidden in the soil,
The staff of life springs forth from the virgin womb.

St. Augustine of Hippo
(AD 354–440)

Let the just rejoice,
for their justifier is born.
Let the sick and infirm rejoice,
for their savior is born.
Let the captives rejoice,
for their redeemer is born.
Let slaves rejoice,
for their master is born.
Let free men rejoice,
for their liberator is born.
Let all Christians rejoice,
for Jesus Christ is born.

St. Bernard of Clairvaux
(AD 1090–1153)

Let your goodness, Lord, appear to us, that we,
made in your image, conform ourselves to it.
In our own strength
we cannot imitate your majesty, power, and wonder,
nor is it fitting for us to try.
But your mercy reaches from the heavens
through the clouds to the earth below.
You have come to us as a small child,
but you have brought us the greatest of all gifts,
the gift of eternal love.
Caress us with your tiny hands,
embrace us with your tiny arms,
and pierce our hearts with your soft, sweet cries.

Pope St. John XXIII
(AD 1881–1963)

Here is a popular Christmas prayer from the recently canonized Pope St. John XXIII.

O sweet Child of Bethlehem,
grant that we may share with all our hearts
in this profound mystery of Christmas.
Put into the hearts of men and women this peace
for which they sometimes seek so desperately
and which you alone can give to them.
Help them to know one another better,
and to live as brothers and sisters,
children of the same Father.
Reveal to them also your beauty, holiness, and purity.
Awaken in their hearts
love and gratitude for your infinite goodness.
Join them all together in your love.
And give us your heavenly peace. Amen.

Pope St. John Paul II
(AD 1920–2005)

Pope St. John Paul II—who was canonized the same day as Pope St. John XXIII—offered this prayer for peace during his public address on Christmas Day, 1994.

Wipe away, Baby Jesus, the tears of children!
Embrace the sick and the elderly!
Move men to lay down their arms
and to draw close in a universal embrace of peace!
Invite the peoples, O merciful Jesus,
to tear down the walls created
by poverty and unemployment,
by ignorance and indifference,
by discrimination and intolerance.
It is you, O Divine Child of Bethlehem,
who save us, freeing us from sin.
It is you who are the true and only Savior,
whom humanity often searches for with uncertainty.
God of peace, gift of peace for all of humanity,
come to live in the heart of every individual
and of every family.
Be our peace and our joy!
Amen!

Ave Maria (Hail Mary)

Probably the second most familiar prayer for Catholics after the Lord's Prayer, the Hail Mary, while not specifically for Christmas, is all about the infant Jesus and his mother. And, rendered in Latin, there are several versions turned into song that are often sung in this season.

The prayer, which dates to early Christianity, is based on two separate lines from Scripture addressed to Mary. The first is spoken by the angel Gabriel at the Annunciation: "Heil, ful of grace; the Lord be with thee" (Lk. 1:28, The Wycliffe Bible, 1395); the second is said by Mary's cousin Elizabeth, who is pregnant with John the Baptist: "Blessed art thou among women, and blessed is the fruit of thy womb" (Lk. 1:42, KJV). At some point in the thirteenth century, the names "Mary" and "Jesus" were added, as if they were needed. The petition— the second half—came later and was codified in the Roman Catechism in the sixteenth century.

There are two widely known sung versions of "Ave Maria." The more familiar was written by Franz Schubert for a secular work based on the epic poem "The Lady of the Lake" and used in Disney's Fantasia. Also widely used is the exquisite setting by Charles Gounod based on a Bach prelude.

Hail Mary, full of grace,
the Lord is with thee.
Blessed art thou amongst women
and blessed is the fruit of thy womb, Jesus.
Holy Mary, Mother of God,
pray for us sinners,
now and at the hour of our death.
Amen.

Ave Maria, gratia plena,
Dominus tecum.
Benedicta tu in mulieribus,
et benedictus fructus ventris tui, Iesus.
Sancta Maria, Mater Dei,
ora pro nobis peccatoribus,
nunc, et in hora mortis nostrae.
Amen.

Essential Christmas Prayers

Christmas Tree Blessings

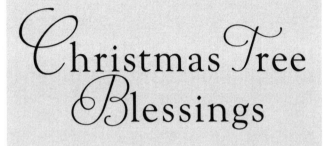

Lord our God,

the heavens are the work of your hands;

the moon and the stars you made,

the earth and the sea,

and every living creature came into being by your word.

And all of us, too.

May this tree bring cheer to this house

through Jesus Christ, your good and holy Son,

who brings life and beauty to us and to our world.

Lighting this tree, we hope in his promise.

Lord, Jesus, encircle this tree with your blessing. May its twinkling lights remind us of the hope and promise of your coming. May we find joy in the memories we share in its tinsel and trimmings. May the presents we place beneath it give rise to an appreciation for the gift of your presence among us. We ask this in your holy name. Amen.

Prayers for
Christmas Eve/
Vigil

God of endless ages, Father of all goodness, we keep vigil for the dawn of salvation and the birth of your Son. With gratitude we recall his humanity, the life he shared with the sons of men. May the power of his divinity help us answer his call to forgiveness and life. We ask this through Christ our Lord. Amen.

God our Father, every year we rejoice as we look forward to this feast of our salvation. May we welcome Christ as our Redeemer, and meet him with confidence when he comes to be our judge, who lives and reigns with you and the Holy Spirit, one God, forever and ever. Amen.

(At midnight)
Father, you make this holy night radiant with the splendor of Jesus Christ our light. We welcome him as Lord, the true light of the world. Bring us to eternal joy in the kingdom of heaven where he lives and reigns with you and the Holy Spirit, one God, forever and ever. Amen.

Lord our God, with the birth of your Son, your glory breaks on the world. Through the night hours of the darkened earth, we your people watch for the coming of your promised Son. As we wait, give us a foretaste of the joy that you will grant us when the fullness of his glory has filled the earth, who lives and reigns with you forever and ever. Amen.

Prayers for Christmas Day

Almighty God and Father of light, a child is born for us and a son is given to us. Your eternal Word leaped down from heaven in the silent watches of the night, and now your Church is filled with wonder at the nearness of her God. Open our hearts to receive his life and increase our vision with the rising of dawn, that our lives may be filled with his glory and his peace, who lives and reigns forever and ever. Amen.

Father, we are filled with the new light by the coming of your Word among us. May the light of faith shine in our words and actions. Grant this through our Lord Jesus Christ, your Son, who lives and reigns with you and the Holy Spirit, one God, forever and ever. Amen.

Glory to God in the highest, and on earth peace to men of good will, alleluia! The Lord has reigned, and he is clothed with beauty. Almighty God, the Savior of the world, who hast nourished us with heavenly food, we give thee thanks for the gift of this bodily refreshment which we have received from thy bountiful mercy. Through Christ our Lord. Amen.

The Word was made flesh, alleluia, alleluia!
And dwelt among us, alleluia, alleluia!

Let the heavens rejoice and the earth be glad,
before the face of the Lord, for he comes.
Bless us, O Lord, and these thy gifts,
which we are about to receive from thy bounty.
Through Christ our Lord.
Amen.

Good Father, bless us, and our parents, our families, and our friends. Open our hearts so that we might know how to receive Jesus with joy, doing always what he asks, and seeing him in all those who are in need of our love. We ask you in the name of Jesus, your beloved Son, who came to bring peace to the world. He lives and reigns with you forever and ever. Amen.

Essential Christmas Prayers

This prayer is for Christmas morning and each morning of the Christmas season.

Almighty God, who hast given us thy only-begotten Son to take our nature upon him, and as at this time to be born of a pure virgin; Grant that we being regenerate, and made thy children by adoption and grace, may daily be renewed by thy Holy Spirit; through the same our Lord Jesus Christ, who liveth and reigneth with thee and the same Spirit ever, one God, world without end. Amen.[7]

Other Prayers
for the
Christmas Season

Lord, in this holy season of prayer and song and laughter, we praise you for the great wonders you have sent us: for shining star and angel's song, for infant's cry in lowly manger. We praise you for the Word made flesh in a little Child. We behold his glory, and are bathed in its radiance.

Be with us as we sing the ironies of Christmas, the incomprehensible comprehended, the poetry made hard fact, the helpless Babe who cracks the world asunder. We kneel before you shepherds, innkeepers, wise men. Help us to rise bigger than we are. Amen.

Almighty God, who hast poured upon us the new light of thine incarnate Word; Grant that the same light enkindled in our hearts may shine forth in our lives; through Jesus Christ our Lord. Amen.[8]

This popular Christmas prayer is often attributed to Robert Louis Stevenson (1850–1894). Whether that's true or not, it is widely shared and inspiring.

Loving Father,
help us remember the birth of Jesus,
that we may share in the song of the angels,
the gladness of the shepherds,
and worship of the wise men.

Close the door of hate
and open the door of love all over the world.
Let kindness come with every gift
and good desires with every greeting.
Deliver us from evil by the blessing which Christ brings,
and teach us to be merry with clear hearts.

May the Christmas morning
make us happy to be thy children,
and Christmas evening bring us to our beds
with grateful thoughts,
forgiving and forgiven,
for Jesus's sake.
Amen.

Essential Christmas Prayers

God Rest You Merry, Gentlemen

"God Rest You Merry, Gentlemen" is one of the earliest Christmas carols—dating from the sixteenth century or earlier—and remains one of the most popular today. It's been performed or incorporated into works by many artists, from Gustav Holst to Bing Crosby to Annie Lennox. It also holds the distinction of being featured in Charles Dickens's *A Christmas Carol*, though he misquotes it:

> The owner of one scant young nose, gnawed and mumbled by the hungry cold as bones are gnawed by dogs, stooped down at Scrooge's keyhole to regale him with a Christmas carol: but at the first sound of God bless you, merry gentleman! May nothing you dismay! Scrooge seized the ruler with such energy of action that the singer fled in terror, leaving the keyhole to the fog and even more congenial frost.[9]

We include the carol in this collection of Christmas prayers because it is really a blessing. You might have noticed the placement of the comma in the title and wondered if you've been saying the carol wrong your whole life, as Dickens did. Yes, most people misunderstand the title phrase and several others. The opening line is not "God rest you, merry gentlemen"; it's "God rest you merry, gentlemen." The word "rest" here is not defined as taking a break or relaxing. Rather, the "rest" in "rest you merry"—a common phrase in the sixteenth century—is from the same root as "the rest," meaning what remains; it means to keep something the way it is. "Merry" is not modifying "gentlemen," but "rest"—it is the state in which the gentlemen are to remain. And "merry" had a more substantial meaning then, having more to do with bounty and joy than the mild happiness we think of today. So, the line "God rest you merry, gentlemen" means something like: May God keep you happy and prosperous, gentlemen.

And one more thing. The very last word of the last line before the final chorus confuses people today as well: "This holy tide of Christmas / All other doth deface." While today we think of effacing as positive and defacing as negative, they originally had similar meanings. This line in the carol means, essentially: This holy time of Christmas outshines all other times to such a degree that they are made irrelevant—erased from importance, so to speak.

With that explanation, here then are several variations on the classic carol.

God Rest You Merry, Gentlemen

—THE COMMON VERSION

Here is the common version today, though often, rather than "God rest you," it is rendered as "God rest ye." This is an archaism—that is, a contrived attempt to make it sound old-fashioned. Versions of this carol dating back hundreds of years, including the one below and the one that follows it, use "you."

God rest you merry, gentlemen,
Let nothing you dismay,
For Jesus Christ our Savior
Was born upon this day,
To save us all from Satan's power
When we were gone astray:
O tidings of comfort and joy,
comfort and joy,
O tidings of comfort and joy.

From God our heavenly Father
A blessed angel came,
And unto certain shepherds
Brought tidings of the same,
How that in Bethlehem was born
The Son of God by name:
O tidings of comfort and joy,
comfort and joy,
O tidings of comfort and joy.

The shepherds at those tidings
Rejoiced much in mind,
And left their flocks a-feeding
In tempest, storm, and wind,
And went to Bethlehem straightway,
This blessed Babe to find:
O tidings of comfort and joy,
comfort and joy,
O tidings of comfort and joy.

But when to Bethlehem they came,
Whereat this Infant lay,
They found Him in a manger,
Where oxen feed on hay;
His mother Mary kneeling,
Unto the Lord did pray:
O tidings of comfort and joy,
comfort and joy,
O tidings of comfort and joy.

Now to the Lord sing praises,
All you within this place,
And with true love and brotherhood
Each other now embrace;
This holy tide of Christmas
All other doth deface:
O tidings of comfort and joy,
comfort and joy,
O tidings of comfort and joy.

Essential Christmas Prayers

God Rest You Merry, Gentlemen
—AN EARLIER VERSION

This version of the carol is the one Charles Dickens would have been misquoting in *A Christmas Carol*. It was recorded by W.B. Sandys, a solicitor by trade and antiquarian by passion. Sandys's 1833 collection of carols, *Christmas Carols Ancient and Modern*, along with Dickens's *A Christmas Carol* a decade later, contributed to the rise in popularity of Christmas in Victorian England. His book was the first appearance in print of "God Rest You Merry, Gentlemen," as well as "Hark the Herald Angels Sing," "The First Noel," and "I Saw Three Ships."

It begins the same as the current version above, but differs substantially in the later verses.

God rest you merry, gentlemen
Let nothing you dismay
For Jesus Christ, our Savior
Was born upon this day,
To save us all from Satan's power
When we were gone astray.
O tidings of comfort and joy,
For Jesus Christ, our Savior, was born on Christmas day.

In Bethlehem, in Jewery,
This blessed babe was born
And laid within a manger
Upon this blessed morn
The which his mother Mary
Nothing did take in scorn.
O tidings of comfort and joy,
For Jesus Christ, our Savior, was born on Christmas day.

From God our Heavenly Father
A blessed Angel came,
And unto certain Shepherds
Brought tidings of the same,
How that in Bethlehem was born
The Son of God by name.
O tidings of comfort and joy,
For Jesus Christ, our Savior, was born on Christmas day.

Fear not, then said the Angel,
Let nothing you affright,
This day is born a Savior
Of virtue, power, and might;
So frequently to vanquish all
The friends of Satan quite.
O tidings of comfort and joy,
For Jesus Christ, our Savior, was born on Christmas day.

Essential Christmas Prayers

The Shepherds at those tidings
Rejoiced much in mind,
And left their flocks a feeding
In tempest, storm, and wind,
And went to Bethlehem straightway,
This blessed babe to find.
O tidings of comfort and joy,
For Jesus Christ, our Savior, was born on Christmas day.

But when to Bethlehem they came,
Whereas this infant lay,
They found him in a manger,
Where oxen feed on hay,
His mother Mary kneeling
Unto the Lord did pray.
O tidings of comfort and joy,
For Jesus Christ, our Savior, was born on Christmas day.

Now to the Lord sing praises,
All you within this place,
And with true love and brotherhood
Each other now embrace;
This holy tide of Christmas
All other doth deface.
O tidings of comfort and joy,
For Jesus Christ, our Savior, was born on Christmas day.

A Christmas Carol

BY DINAH MARIA CRAIK

Dinah Maria Craik wrote the poem "A Christmas Carol" near the end of her life in the 1880s. The daughter of a poor preacher, Craik had established herself as a novelist and poet and married George Lillie Craik, a partner in the Macmillan & Company publishing house, becoming a popular member of the London social scene. This poem is, of course, a riff on the popular carol "God Rest You Merry, Gentlemen" and includes both common errors: the archaism "ye" and the misplaced comma—in fact, the poem does not work without the comma being in the wrong place. The middle stanza about children has survived as a popular quote.

God rest ye, merry gentlemen; let nothing you dismay,
For Jesus Christ, our Savior, was born on Christmas-day.
The dawn rose red o'er Bethlehem, the stars shone through
    the gray,
When Jesus Christ, our Savior, was born on Christmas-day.

God rest ye, little children; let nothing you affright,
For Jesus Christ, your Savior, was born this happy night;
Along the hills of Galilee the white flocks sleeping lay,
When Christ, the Child of Nazareth, was born on Christmas-
    day.

Essential Christmas Prayers

God rest ye, all good Christians; upon this blessed morn
The Lord of all good Christians was of a woman born:
Now all your sorrows He doth heal, your sins He takes
    away;
For Jesus Christ, our Savior, was born on Christmas-day.

Other Christmas Prayers in Song

As with Advent hymns, some Christmas carols are prayers put to music. Here are a few other beloved Christmas prayer songs.

Puer natus est

"Puer natus est" is an introit—an accompaniment to the entrance procession—used in Roman Catholic Christmas Day services. While this prayer has a specific liturgical role, it could be a lovely Christmas prayer for any occasion. It is based on Isaiah 9:6, "For a child has been born for us, a son given to us; authority rests upon his shoulders; and he is named Wonderful Counselor, Mighty God, Everlasting Father, Prince of Peace"(NRSV).

Puer natus est nobis
Et filius datus est nobis
Cuius imperium super humerum eius
Et vocabitur nomen eius
Magni consilii Angelus

Cantate Domino canticum novum
Quia mirabilia fecit

Gloria Patri, et Filio, et Spiritui Sancto. Sicut erat in principio, et nunc, et semper, in secula seculorum. Amen.

A boy is born to us,
and a son is given to us,
upon whose shoulders authority rests,
and His name will be called
"The Angel of Great Counsel."

> Sing to the Lord a new song,
> because he has done the miraculous.

Glory to the Father, and to the Son, and to the Holy Spirit. As it was in the beginning, and is now, and always will be, in every human generation. Amen.

The Sussex Carol

This song is by Luke Waddinge, Bishop of Ferns, Ireland, published in his little book, *A Smale Garland of Pious and Godly Songs, Composed by a Devout Man for the Solace of his Friends and Neighbours in their Afflictions* (Ghent, 1684). Bishop Waddinge was related to Franciscan friar Luke Wadding; Jesuit missionary to Mexico Michael Wadding, known there as Miguel Godinez; and Jesuit theologian and chancellor of the University of Prague Peter Wadding. His little book is credited with encouraging the tradition of carol singing in Ireland. The version known today was collected and arranged by Ralph Vaughan Williams in the early twentieth century.[10]

> On Christmas night all Christians sing
> To hear the news the angels bring.
> News of great joy, news of great mirth,
> News of our merciful King's birth.
>
> Then why should men on earth be so sad,
> Since our Redeemer made us glad,
> When from our sin he set us free,
> All for to gain our liberty?
>
> When sin departs before His grace,
> Then life and health come in its place.
> Angels and men with joy may sing
> All for to see the new-born King.

All out of darkness we have light,
Which made the angels sing this night:
"Glory to God and peace to men,
Now and for evermore!" Amen.

Jesus, the Father's Only Son

"Christe, Redemptor omnium" is a sixth-century hymn traditionally used for Vespers during the Christmas season. This English translation is from John Mason Neale (1818-1866).

Jesu, the Father's only Son,
Whose death for all redemption won;
Before the worlds of God most high
Begotten all ineffably.

The Father's light and splendor Thou,
Their endless hope to Thee that bow;
Accept the prayers and praise today
That through the world Thy servants pray.

Salvation's author, call to mind
How, taking form of humankind,
Born of a virgin undefiled,
Thou in man's flesh becam'st a child.

Thus testifies the present day,
Through every year in long array,
That Thou, salvation's source alone,
Proceedest from the Father's throne.

Whence sky, and stars, and sea's abyss,
And earth, and all that therein is,
Shall still, with laud and carol meet,
The Author of Thine advent greet.

And we who, by Thy precious blood
From sin redeemed, are marked for God,
On this the day that saw Thy birth,
Sing the new song of ransomed earth.

For that Thine advent glory be,
O Jesu, virgin born, to Thee;
With Father, and with Holy Ghost,
From men and from the heavenly host.

Essential Christmas Prayers

Song of Simeon (Nunc dimittis)

In the account of Jesus's birth in Luke, we find the story of Simeon. The Holy Spirit has told this elderly man that he will not die before he sees the Messiah. It goes on to say the Spirit led Simeon to be at the temple on the day Mary and Joseph brought the baby Jesus there for a ceremony. On seeing the baby, "Simeon took him in his arms and praised God, saying, 'Master, now you are dismissing your servant in peace, according to your word; for my eyes have seen your salvation, which you have prepared in the presence of all peoples, a light for revelation to the Gentiles and for glory to your people Israel'" (Lk. 2:28–32, NRSV). While the dismissal Simeon referred to was his own death, these words from the story of the birth of Jesus have become the canticle used at the end of each day—Night Prayer or Compline, and sometimes Evening Prayer. While the Presentation of Christ in the Temple is celebrated with Candlemas on February 2, it is a fitting closing prayer for this collection.

A version for the Order for Daily Evening Prayer in the 1928 Book of Common Prayer:[11]

> LORD, now lettest thou thy servant depart in peace, according to thy word.
> For mine eyes have seen thy salvation,
> Which thou hast prepared before the face of all people;
> To be a light to lighten the Gentiles, and to be the glory of thy people Israel.

A version for the Roman Office of Compline:[12]

Now, O my Lord, let Thy servant depart in peace, according to Thy word; for mine eyes have seen Thy compassion, which Thou hast prepared for the salvation of all peoples, a light to all nations, and glory to Thy people Israel.

And the Vulgate Latin:

> *Nunc dimittis servum tuum, Domine,*
> *secundum verbum tuum in pace:*
> *Quia viderunt oculi mei salutare tuum*
> *Quod parasti ante faciem omnium populorum:*
> *Lumen ad revelationem gentium,*
> *et gloriam plebis tuae Israel.*

$\mathcal{S}$*ources*

1   Christina Georgina Rossetti, *Time Flies: A Reading Diary* (London: Society for Promoting Christian Knowledge, 1885).

2   Martin Luther, in *Lyra Germanica: Hymns for the Sundays and Chief Festivals of the Christian Year*, trans. Catherine Winkworth (London: Longman, Brown, Green and Longmans, 1855), 13–14.

3   Henry van Dyke, *The Spirit of Christmas* (New York: Charles Scribner's Sons, 1905).

4   Ibid.

5   Book of Common Prayer as adopted by the General Convention of 1928 and amended by subsequent Conventions.

6   *The English Hymnal*, ed. Percy Dearmer and Ralph Vaughan Williams (London: Oxford University Press, 1906).

7   Book of Common Prayer, 1928.

8   Ibid.

9   Charles Dickens, *A Christmas Carol* (Brewster, MA: Paraclete Press, 2016), 19.

10   Ralph Vaughan Williams, *Eight Traditional English Carols* (London: Stainer & Bell, 1919).

11   Book of Common Prayer, 1928.

12   *The Ante-Nicene Fathers: Translations of the Writings of the Fathers Down to A.D. 325*, ed. The Rev. Alexander Roberts, DD, and James Donaldson, LLD (New York: Charles Scribner's Sons, 1903).

About Paraclete Press

Who We Are

Paraclete Press is a publisher of books, recordings, and DVDs on Christian spirituality. Our publishing represents a full expression of Christian belief and practice—from Catholic to Evangelical, from Protestant to Orthodox.

We are the publishing arm of the Community of Jesus, an ecumenical monastic community in the Benedictine tradition. As such, we are uniquely positioned in the marketplace without connection to a large corporation and with informal relationships to many branches and denominations of faith.

What We Are Doing

PARACLETE PRESS BOOKS | Paraclete publishes books that show the richness and depth of what it means to be Christian. Although Benedictine spirituality is at the heart of all that we do, we publish books that reflect the Christian experience across many cultures, time periods, and houses of worship. We publish books that nourish the vibrant life of the church and its people.

We have several different series, including the bestselling Paraclete Essentials and Paraclete Giants series of classic texts in contemporary English; Voices from the Monastery—men and women monastics writing about living a spiritual life today; award-winning poetry; bestselling gift books for children on the occasions of baptism and first communion; and the Active Prayer Series that brings creativity and liveliness to any life of prayer.

MOUNT TABOR BOOKS | Paraclete's newest series, Mount Tabor Books, focuses on the arts and literature as well as liturgical worship and spirituality, and was created in conjunction with the Mount Tabor Ecumenical Centre for Art and Spirituality in Barga, Italy.

PARACLETE RECORDINGS | From Gregorian chant to contemporary American choral works, our recordings celebrate the best of sacred choral music composed through the centuries that create a space for heaven and earth to intersect. Paraclete Recordings is the record label representing the internationally acclaimed choir Gloriæ Dei Cantores, praised for their "rapt and fathomless spiritual intensity" by *American Record Guide*; the Gloriæ Dei Cantores Schola, specializing in the study and performance of Gregorian chant; and the other instrumental artists of the Arts Empowering Life Foundation.

Paraclete Press is also privileged to be the exclusive North American distributor of the recordings of the Monastic Choir of St. Peter's Abbey in Solesmes, France, long considered to be a leading authority on Gregorian chant.

PARACLETE VIDEO | Our DVDs offer spiritual help, healing, and biblical guidance for a broad range of life issues including grief and loss, marriage, forgiveness, facing death, bullying, addictions, Alzheimer's, and spiritual formation.

Learn more about us at our website:
www.paracletepress.com or phone us
toll-free at 1.800.451.5006

SCAN
TO
READ
MORE

Also Available from Paraclete Press . . .

A Christmas Carol

CHARLES DICKENS
978-1-61261-839-5
$9.99 Paperback – Fully illustrated

𝓜ost of us know the story, but perhaps you or someone you love has never read the original novella — a story that changed the English-speaking world's understanding of what it means to celebrate Christmas.

This new edition of *A Christmas Carol* is a lovely gift book for anyone who doesn't yet own the timeless classic. Who can resist the story of the bad-tempered Ebenezer Scrooge's transformation into a kinder and more loving version of himself? The visiting ghosts of past, present, and future? The deeply good Bob Cratchit and his son Tiny Tim? Create or revive a tradition and gather to read this classic tale each and every year.

This new edition is beautifully published and economically priced. It's a lovely gift book for anyone who doesn't yet own this classic tale that should be read each year as Christmas comes 'round.

Includes illustrations from the original 1843 edition!

"Christmas Carol" paperback recaptures charm of 1st edition
—Read a review on MassLive: http://bit.ly/2vlexu8

Available through your local bookseller or through Paraclete Press: www.paracletepress.com; 1-800-451-5006